How to Turn your PhD into a Book

Dr Hilary Potter

How to Turn your PhD into a Book

a pocket guide

PETER LANG

Oxford · Berlin · Bruxelles · Chennai · Lausanne · New York

Bibliographic information published by the Deutsche Nationalbibliothek.
The German National Library lists this publication in the German National Bibliography; detailed bibliographic data is available on the Internet at http://dnb.d-nb.de.

A catalogue record for this book is available from the British Library.

Library of Congress Cataloging-in-Publication Data
Names: Potter, Hilary (Hilary Jane) author
Title: How to turn your PhD into a book : a pocket guide/Hilary Potter.
Description: Oxford ; New York : Peter Lang, [2026] | Includes bibliographical references and index.
Identifiers: LCCN 2025049356 (print) | LCCN 2025049357 (ebook) | ISBN 9781803749419 paperback | ISBN 9781803749426 pdf | ISBN 9781803749433 epub
Subjects: LCSH: Scholarly publishing--Handbooks, manuals, etc.
Classification: LCC Z286.S37 P68 2028 (print) | LCC Z286.S37 (ebook)
LC record available at https://lccn.loc.gov/2025049356
LC ebook record available at https://lccn.loc.gov/2025049357

Cover design by Peter Lang Group AG

ISBN 978-1-80374-941-9 (Print)
ISBN 978-1-80374-942-6 (ePDF)
ISBN 978-1-80374-943-3 (ePUB)
DOI 10.3726/b23556

Published by Peter Lang Ltd, Oxford, United Kingdom

info@peterlang.com

This publication has been peer reviewed.

www.peterlang.com

Contact for General Product Safety Regulation (GPSR): gpsr@peterlang.com

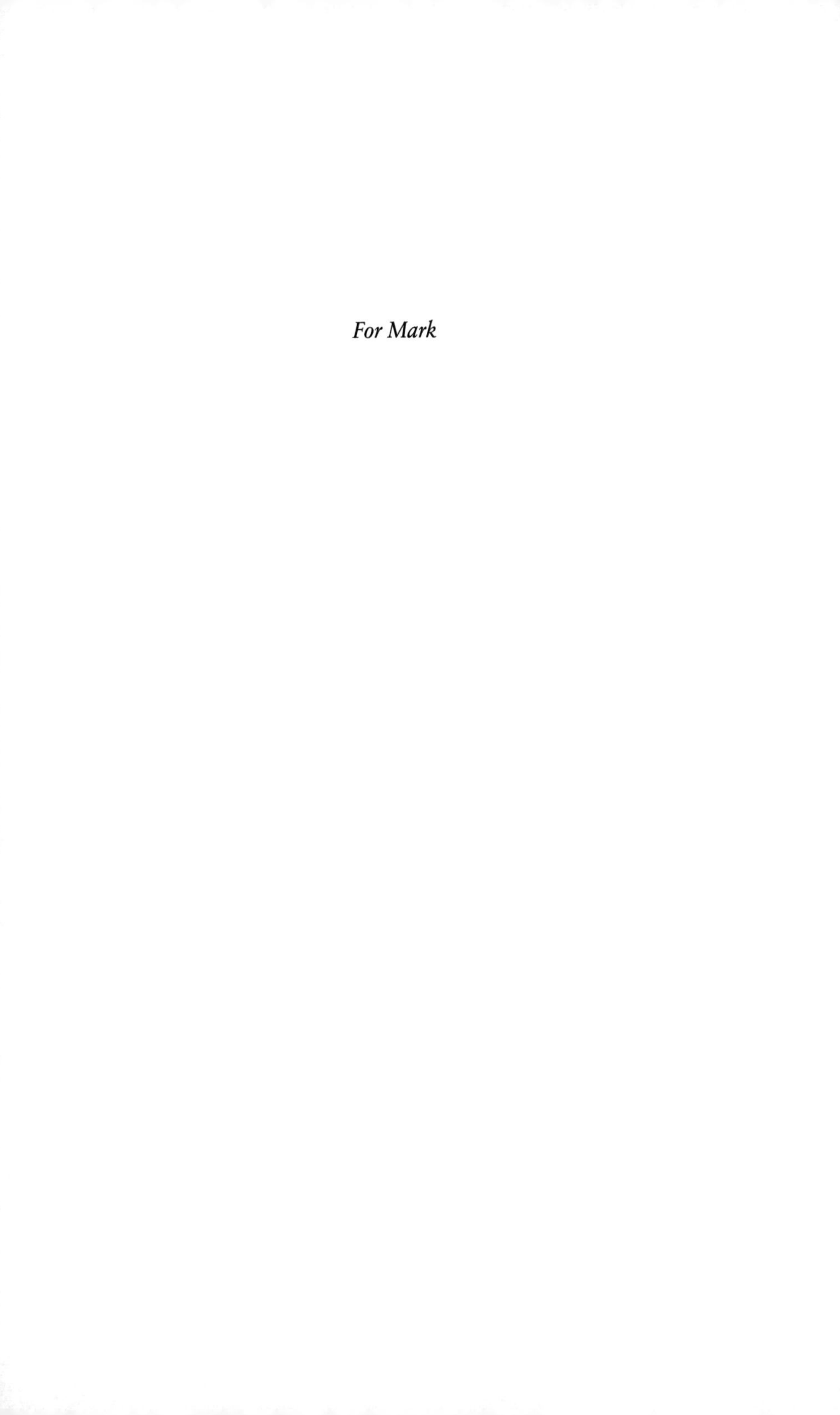

For Mark

Contents

Preface

I'd always wanted to write a book, to see it in a bookshop and think, yes, I did that. By the time I had finished my PhD, however, the last thing I wanted to do was start writing again. I just wasn't ready. I did still want to write at least one book. So, I took some time out, and then the urge to write came back.

It took me a lot longer than I had originally thought it would, but just over three and a half years after I started, two jobs, and two house moves later, publication day finally arrived, albeit a little delayed by one minor flood and my being away when the box of author copies arrived in the post. I got a tingling feeling of excitement when I finally opened the box containing my book, and a feeling of contentedness, too.

[HP]

Congratulations. You've successfully completed your PhD. That is a huge achievement. So, what next? At this point you may already have decided to turn your PhD into a book, or you may just be thinking about it.

How to Turn Your PhD into a Book is designed to help you every step of the way. It enables you to build your own bespoke guide from the activities contained within these pages. If you are wondering why I am getting you to do the work, rather than just telling you what to do, the answer is quite simply to engender your sense of authorial agency, for you to be, and to feel, able to write your book with the confidence and authority of the expert you are in your chosen subject.

Turning your PhD into a book is sometimes described as re-writing. You are doing more than that. In fact, re-writing is an unhelpful way to think about it, implying as it does that you only need to revise what you have been working on. There is a crucial distinction to be made here. Revising would imply there is no fundamental change to your work, that it has the same objective and audience.

Turning your PhD into a book is in fact a re-purposing of your PhD, or parts of it. You are doing so for different reasons and for new audiences. This is also why it will differ from the books you go on to write in the future. Every other book you write will have a different source of origin, one that is decoupled from obtaining a higher degree. It is precisely the point of origin that makes turning your PhD into a book a challenging endeavour. You do not want it to read like a PhD thesis, nor will your reader want to feel as though they are your examiner, yet it needs to be scholarly and authoritative.

So how do you achieve this balance between scholarly and authoritative without your work reading like a PhD? The steps in this book are intended to guide you on precisely that. As an analogy, let us use that of a **journey**. Your PhD thesis is your starting point; your destination is your book. Using the activities, guidance and tips provided here, you are going to map out your own route, working towards it with every step you take. As with any journey, you might double back, take diversions, swerve obstacles in your way. You may decide to do some of these steps side by side, a little like listening to music whilst travelling. *How to Turn Your PhD into a Book* provides a suggested route, but you are at liberty to use as much or as little of it as you like and to play around with the order in which you do things. The idea is that you use this as a map, but you plot it to suit you and your future book.

There are thirty steps in this book. They incorporate a range of activities, which are complemented by accompanying examples. That is not to suggest there are definitive answers, rather, the examples function as prompts for your own thinking. Each activity has an accompanying rationale explaining the reason and purpose for what I ask you to do. By offering you an understanding of the reason for each activity you become more than a passive recipient of knowledge – you can actively engage with it in an informed way. There is real value in understanding what you are doing, and why. In addition, there is merit to being hands on, in *doing* as well as *reading*. Of course, you can just read and think, equally, you can be entirely creative in how you engage with this content. That decision is yours to make, and you are best served by doing what feels right to you. *How to Turn Your PhD into a Book* is designed so that you can dip in and out of it as it suits you and come back to any section as often as you wish. It is your companion as you write your book.

I have intentionally included other voices in this book, those of colleagues from across a range of fields and stages in their writing journey. Their quotes, interspersed throughout these pages, bring perspectives in addition to my own. You may recognise your own experiences within them, or learn from them, all of which is designed to help you with your writing.

How to Turn Your PhD into a Book is about the process of writing but has also been written with the awareness that turning your PhD into a book takes place in conjunction with many other competing factors that will also inform your experience. It therefore seeks to encapsulate this process as a whole.

This book is aimed primarily but not exclusively at scholars from across the Arts and Humanities and, I hope, whatever your subject specialism, this book will give you confidence and help you to turn your PhD into a book.

Step-by-Step

Step 1. Finding reasons to write a book

As you embark on this journey it is worth thinking about why you are undertaking it. This is helpful for practical reasons, as you'll see over the next steps, but also for motivation throughout. If you are clear why you want to do this, that will bolster you on days where you find working on the book difficult. Let's get straight into an activity.

Activity: *Reasons for writing a book based on your PhD*

This is a reflective activity designed for future use in maintaining motivation throughout the writing process from start to finish.

Write out as many reasons as you can think of about why you aim to write a book. Be as creative as you wish.

Keep it somewhere accessible and refer to it as often as you need to help with focus and motivation.

There are no set answers to this question, your ideas can be built over time. Although far from exhaustive, these suggestions may provide some inspiration.

Now you've got your reasons, you're in a good position to take the next step. Just remember this doesn't have to be your definitive list; you can come back to it at any time and add further reasons.

Reasons for Writing a Book

- To influence your academic subject field
- To fulfil a long-held desire to write a book
- To use in teaching
- To aid career development – publishing is integral to Higher Education – a book makes you more competitive
- To share your research beyond your supervisors and examiners – a lot of work has gone into the PhD, this is a chance to bring that to a wider audience
- To establish a reputation in the field for the books you will write after this one

Step 2. Planning publications from your PhD

Does the fact that you wrote one PhD automatically equate to writing one book based on it? The answer is not necessarily. Yes, it can, but don't feel that you must limit yourself to one book. You might have already published something or have something pending, be it from your PhD or in the form of a review. This experience will be beneficial to you, making you more familiar with publishing processes and writing for publication, so that it may feel that a book is a natural next progression in your publication journey. Whether or not this is the case, you may have parts of your PhD that lend themselves better to a different kind of output, such as a journal article, creative practice, or public engagement activity. Journal articles have long been a staple of academic publishing and are usually quicker to produce, making them helpful in the competitive higher education job market. Creative practice is increasingly gaining traction in its relevant fields, and public engagement is important in developing pathways to future impact and to knowledge exchange, which are also key skills. You might decide that a book is not right for you in this instance. That's ok, too. You can still use the resources in this book to map out what you want to do with your PhD. Any, and all these answers are absolutely fine.

There are a number of factors you can consider when planning publications from your PhD:

- The norms of your field.
- The career trajectory you are aiming for and how publications factor into that.

- Turnaround times: an article may take less time to write but the time between submission and publication will vary depending on the journal.
- Mode of dissemination and audience reach. You may, for example, prefer to write something for the media or contribute to a podcast, which in turn may generate interest in your future book.
- A PhD is far more substantial than an article, so even if you take one aspect of it and repackage it for an article, it is only going to be a small part of it.
- Consider aspects that you could not include in your PhD, and whether these could be repurposed either for an article, podcast, media contribution, or indeed as part of your book.

None of these factors means you have to make a binary choice between book or another publication: they serve the purpose of helping you decide on the range of publications you may want to work towards.

Activity: *Calculating whether 1 PhD = 1 book*

This activity Is designed to help you decide how to make best use of your PhD in terms of publishable content.

Using the reasons that you listed in Step 1 for writing a book, and the points listed earlier, ask yourself if you could turn your PhD into just one book or could you use some of it for an article, podcast, media contribution, for example?

Once you have calculated your publication plans, reflect on, and note down what you plan to focus on and in what order.

By taking the time to answer this question, you're preparing for the next steps whilst beginning to create publication plans.

Step 3. Breaking up with your PhD

One of the trickiest skills in turning your PhD into a book is making it sufficiently academic without it reading like a PhD. Some of that comes down to writing strategies, but some of it is linked to the relationship you develop with your PhD thesis over time. You spent a long time crafting it, after all. The word **relationship** is key here. You'll have already gone through various different stages in it just to get to the PhD. Now you need to go one step further. Imagine your PhD as a person, and you're going to break up with it via letter. This does not mean you'll never have anything to do with your PhD again, or that it is now irrelevant, far from it. This activity aims to help you to move on to the next stage in your writing life, to start to move away from the PhD and into book-writing mode.

> Writing a 'break-up' letter to my PhD was a surprisingly cathartic process. It helps you to let go of perfectionism, reflect on the journey, and redefine your relationship with the work going forward. It's both a playful and a profound activity to find closure with the PhD process and move forward with fresh energy for writing something different.
>
> [LE]

Activity: *Dear PhD thesis, I'm leaving you …*

This is a creative activity designed to be cathartic in the first instance, leading you to articulate how your book will differ from your PhD, bringing you some clarity of thought and purpose.

Take a sheet of paper and write a letter to your PhD thesis, effectively breaking up with it. You can tell it all the good things about it, but also what you disliked, what you don't want to deal with anymore. You could do this as a list if you prefer, but the advantage of a 'Dear PhD' letter is that it gives you creative distance. It can be tongue-in-cheek, light-touch, or heartfelt, but approaching it in an informal way helps unlock your thinking, which in turn liberates your thinking about what you would like to get out of the book and what you really don't. Once you've written the letter, you can then think about how you structure your book. The letter is yours to write, it is as personal and individual as your thesis, there's no minimum or maximum word count, no referencing required, really you can use any format you want, the decisions are all yours, but here's an example to get you thinking.

My dearest PhD,
Well, where to begin? I guess, by saying how immensely proud I am of you, and of all we've achieved together. As I sit and look at you, all neatly bound, encased in a maroon-coloured cover, with your gold lettering, I know the outer appearance shows only what you are, but it is so far removed from our story. It is unable to tell what went on between, around and because of those sheets of neatly printed and bound paper. We know it to be a story of twists and turns, depths of despair, flashes of inspiration, times of joy amongst the hours spent together, the underdogs who came good in the end.

Perhaps, if I'd not rushed in eager to get started, and waited instead for full funding, we might have had an easier time of it financially at least, but then, the fact that we got there whilst juggling jobs, moving away and writing at a distance, tells me so much about strength, endurance and capabilities, that I'm more than the sum of you, my dearest thesis. It tells me that you were my inspiration, a physical, tangible testament of overcoming the odds. You really were an experience of two halves – the difficult start. We endured a changing secondary supervisory relationship, whilst our lead endured loyally with us, and then the experience became that which it always should have been, with a marvellous supervisory team. We had a viva that seemed to go by in a flash, truly in inverse proportion to the time it took to write you. Then we had our graduation with all the happiness and celebrating that goes with it, including hugs from random strangers!

Yet, things need to change between us. It is not so much the end of the road, as a junction on it where I follow a new route. There is a different path for you. You become an inspiration for others in your own right, for the others who read you as you are, for the students who will meet you when I bring you to class. However, I need a new relationship with a new book. You're my stimulus, but you cannot be its duplicate, nor it yours. It will be shorter for a start, and hopefully it will not take as long to write or be as costly, though it will cost. Above all, I'll not be falling over myself to justify every little thing I say. It'll give an air of authority and expertise beyond what I could demonstrate through you. Nor will there be so much name dropping, sure there will be enough, but it'll be less like a sycophant vying to be noticed and approved of.

I'm also going to drop some aspects. You needed to have them, but the new book doesn't, so I'm not going to hold it back for fear that someone may say 'oh but why didn't you include this or that'.

This isn't the end of things for us. You remain so important to me and will always be a part of the person I have become, but this letter marks a moving forward into a new era, into unchartered waters for me, an adventure of its own kind, just as it was when I began us. For us it is a distancing from one another.

So, all that remains is for me to thank-you, my dearest PhD thesis, for everything that has gone before and for everything that is to come as a result. I'm not saying goodbye, more auf Wiedersehen.

Step 4. Changing your title and why you should

You've probably got a great title for your PhD and the prospect of changing it may seem unwelcome right now. However, it will need to change. This does not have to happen immediately – you can change it as you move through the process. You might be wondering why. There are three broad considerations here: **searchability, marketability** and the **psychological effect**.

Let's focus on **searchability** first. This is important in making your book findable via a web search. Suppose for a moment that you retained your PhD title for your book. The chances are when you search online, the book will be the first hit, but it will be followed by your PhD. Most countries now have the requirement of archiving PhDs electronically in institutional or national repositories, like Ethos in the UK and ProQuest in the USA. Imagine now you are a potential reader. Remember, ask yourself honestly, what is the likelihood you would buy the book knowing you could download a version of it for free?

Suggesting a title change may sound cynical, as if I'm encouraging you to be deceptive. I'm not. The PhD gives your book a validity – ideas are tried and tested through the PhD, but your book is not your thesis. They are related, but they have different purposes and different audiences. You couldn't reasonably expect someone to buy your PhD thesis, but you can expect people to pay for a book. This brings us to the second reason for changing your title, **marketability.** You may feel your PhD title is so good you can't change it, but that's your perspective, rather than your prospective reader's. You're invested in that title because it is about your PhD and achieving that higher degree. Your readers won't be invested in it the same way. University librarians will form a proportion of your future potential buyers. It is their job to source resources, shaping their offer to their members' needs and interests. If a book title mirrors a PhD title, it will not immediately suggest it is worth investing in. To attract readers to your book, they first need to notice it, and then they need to be interested enough to consider it. Your title needs to appeal, to hook your reader in.

Let's turn to the third reason for changing your title – the **psychological effect** it has on you, the author, and on your writing. It is easy to overlook this – small details can make a big difference. If you keep the same title for your book, you can – without realising it – become bowed down by the ideas of writing to pass, to be approved of, to reach an aim, an educational goal. Instead, you need to write as the authority you have become by successfully completing your PhD. Making a small change can reap benefits for you. Changing your title is no easy task. That is why in the next activity you can first analyse mine before turning your attention to your own in the follow-up activity.

Activity: *Comparative title analysis*

This analytical activity is designed to help you think about title writing and how you can apply the lessons learned to your own title.

Read both titles and answer the following questions.

PhD: The Dynamics of German Remembering. The Rosenstrasse Protest in Historical Debate and Cultural Representation

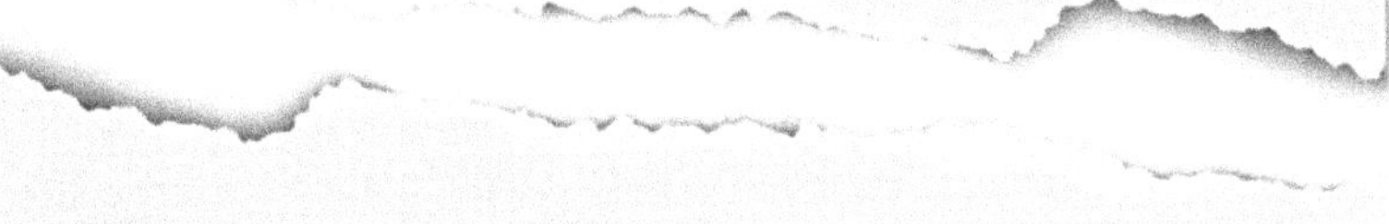

Book: Remembering Rosenstrasse: History, Memory, Identity in Contemporary Germany

- What do you notice about the two titles?
- Why are the differences important?
- What points can you take away from this analysis for your own book title?

Your notes

You might note the following:

The PhD title	The book title
- *is long*	- *is catchier*
- *indicates a power dynamic*	- *is more concise*
- *provides a high-level summary of the content*	- *tells you what it is about*
- *doesn't indicate a timeframe*	- *uses alliteration and triples*

Summary

The differences occur because of genre or style conventions between a piece of work written for examination purposes and a piece of work written for wider, public dissemination. Each title needs to fit to the respective styles. The PhD title above amounts to a summary of the content, telling the examiners precisely what it is about. The book title by contrast is designed to be broader, to appeal to a potential reader's general interests, sparking their curiosity, making them want to know more, thereby making it more appealing, more sellable.

Activity: *Planning your title change*

Changing your title may appear to be easy but in practice can be difficult. This activity is designed to help you do that. Follow the steps sequentially.

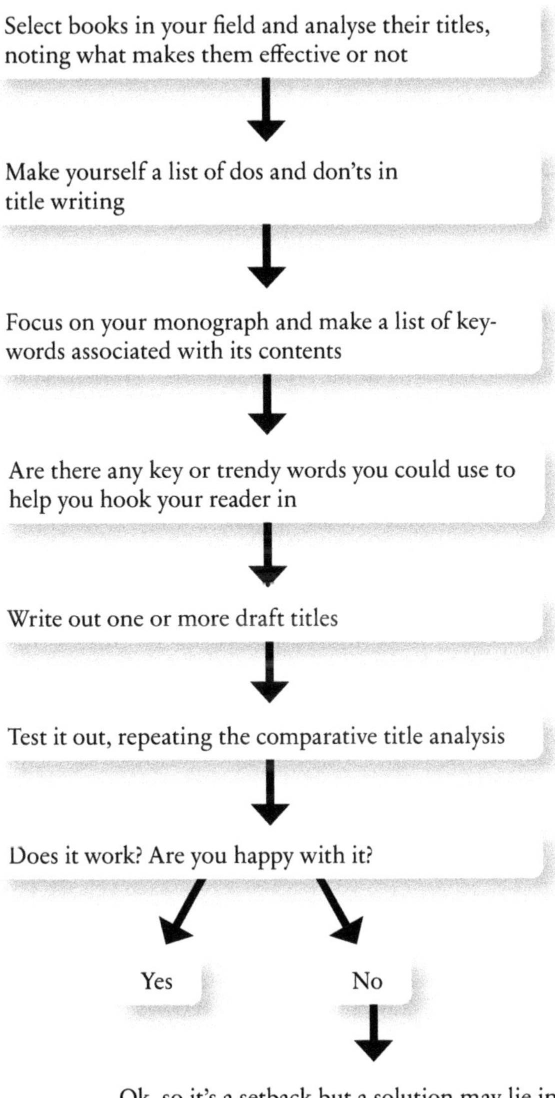

Tip: Try going analogue for this, using pen/pencil and paper – writing by hand can help thinking and creativity.

Step 5. Structuring your book

Now you've completed Steps 3 and 4, you are able to think about the structure of your book. You may find that this is something you return to as you write. That is entirely normal and can make for a better book. It may be that your book structure mirrors that of your PhD closely, particularly if there is a chronology running through it that prevents you from making significant structural alterations. It may be that you add one or more additional chapters or remove some. It may be that you restructure it significantly. A book allows for greater flexibility than a PhD thesis. Now is your opportunity to make changes. You'll need to reduce the overall word count, and reshaping can help to do that.

Activity: *Chop and change*

This is a creative activity designed to challenge and test your manuscript's proposed structure. By doing this you are clearing your mind of the structure you are familiar with, allowing you to see other possible patterns by making the headings more visual and tangible in a way they are not on an on-screen document. It gives you the basis for the next follow-on activity.

- i. Using pieces of card or paper, write out your chapter headings
- ii. Move them around to consider a different order
- iii. Next create an imaginary pitch explaining and justifying your structure

You could write this out or if you can talk it through with a colleague, mentor or friend, you'll benefit from their questions or suggestions. You may also find you change chapter titles and subheadings too, though this should be a more iterative process as you write.

Structural changes will not happen in one sitting; they'll continue evolving with your book. Nevertheless, these are techniques to get you thinking and, at the same time, to stop you feeling as though you must structure in deference to your PhD.

Step 6. Identifying your readers

The key to writing anything is knowing your audience. You need to write differently for different audiences and different text types. The same is true when you are effectively re-purposing something for a new audience, as you are with your book.

In the following set of activities, you are going to look at your different readers, comparing your thesis audience with your book audience, performing an analysis of their purposes, your reader needs. In the process, you will identify changes you need to make, be they structural or stylistic, which you can then use to help you in writing your book. The purpose of this is to give you targeted actions for your writing process that move you towards your goal, while moving your book away from reading like a thesis.

Activity: *PhD analysis*

This is a knowledge-building activity designed to generate a focused understanding of the changes you'll be making as you develop your PhD into a book, and why.

By performing this analysis, you will be better placed to understand how and why it needs to be changed to be ready for publication.

Analyse your PhD and populate the accompanying template with your findings. You only need to make a few notes, and key words will suffice, whatever works best for you.

PhD readers

What your readers were looking for

Purpose of the PhD

Effect of the above on style

Effect of the above on your thinking

As this analysis addresses your PhD, there are no set answers. However, you may find your analysis looks something like this:

PhD readers

- *Supervisor(s)*
- *Examiners*

What your readers were looking for

- *Originality*
- *Academic rigour*
- *Fits with conventions*
- *Justifications with reference to other scholars*
- *Methodological sophistication*
- *Proof of expertise in the subject*

Purpose of the PhD

- *To obtain your doctorate*
- *To prove you have fulfilled all requirements*
- *To prepare for a career in academia*

Effect of the above on style

- *Highly detailed*
- *Thorough*
- *Defensive, justifying every statement*
- *Thoroughly referenced, may have detailed footnotes*

Effect of the above on your thinking

Seeking approval can lead to a deferential tone, defensive style

Activity: *Scaling change*

This is a visualisation activity designed to give you perspective on the task ahead.

i. To what extent will your future book readers want the same things as your PhD readers?
ii. To answer this question, draw yourself a sliding scale (1 = identical, 5= far removed) such as the one below.
iii. Mark the point on the scale below where your book will best fit.

Note: You can amend this at any time as you develop your book.

PhD to book scale

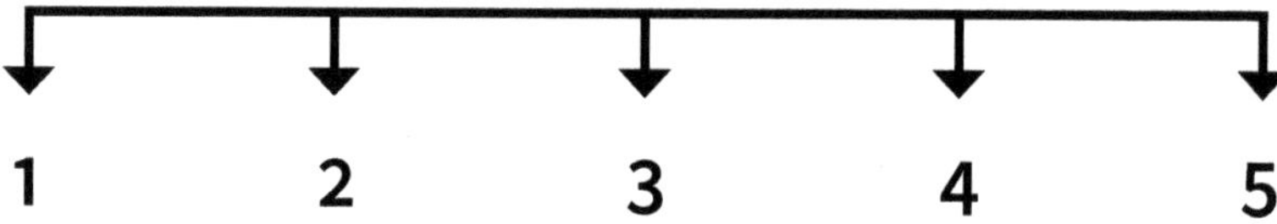

Activity: *Identifying your future book readers*

This is a reflective activity designed to make you focus on your future readership. It provides the basis for the subsequent two activities that follow. Make a list of your potential future readers.

Future readers of my book

It might look something like this:

Future readers of my book

Academics in my and related fields

Students – undergraduate/postgraduate in my and related fields

Practitioners

General/lay audience interested in the topic

Activity: *Visualise your readers*

This is a creative activity designed to help you think about your different readers, and what features they will be looking for in your work. Now you've thought about who your new readers are likely to be, try to visualise them as a way of helping to conceptualise their needs. The idea is that you will then be able to make informed choices about the changes you need to make in your book compared with the thesis. This will be completed as a separate activity.

i. Take a sheet of paper
ii. Draw a figure – a stick figure is absolutely fine
iii. Now put yourself in their position

Now imagine:

- their lives
- why they might be reading you
- what else their working life may include and how this may impact on what they want to get from your book, and crucially what they **won't** want

Note: If you wish, you can make a plasticine/cardboard model instead. Be as creative as you like.

This might seem like a long, time-consuming task, but it's valuable in the long run. It might look something like this:

Imagined reader 1: An academic in my field

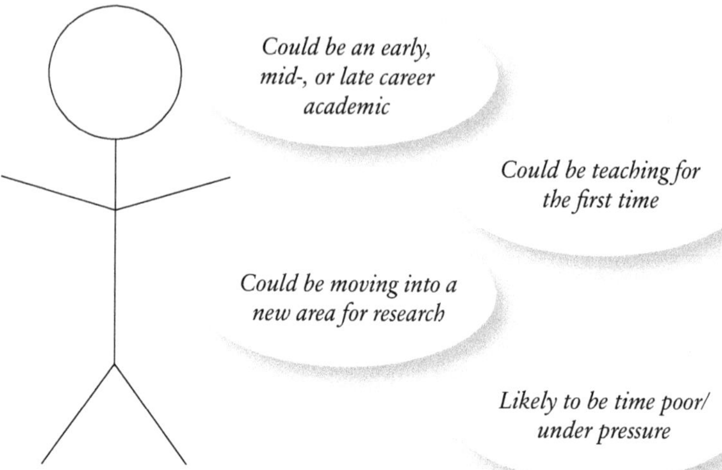

Findings based on imagined reader 1

Will be looking for:

- informed writing
- clear and concise argumentation
- indication or usable summary of method or methods employed
- a useful bibliography
- an index

Will not want:

- to read something that gives the impression they have to mark or examine it
- to hunt through the text looking for your argument

Imagined reader 2: An undergraduate student in my field

Likely to be time poor and juggling conflicting deadlines

Likely reading for a course or an assignment

May have imposter syndrome

Reading to fill gaps in their knowledge – may have little knowledge of your topic and its associated terminology

Going to have less knowledge than you and may not be well developed in critical and analytical skills

Findings based on imagined reader 2

Will be looking for:

- Clear argumentation so they can follow your explanations and analysis
- Good references they can use/cite
- A good glossary and a clear explanation of terms used

Will not want:

- Jargon
- A long, dense text where the main arguments and explanations are hidden – in this instance they are likely to give up, meaning that you won't be read.
- Very long sentences with multiple clauses.

Now repeat this process for each of your imagined readers.

Tip: Your own reader experience can also be useful to you – all good writers, after all, are also readers. You can think about the books you most enjoyed while writing your PhD, analyse your own reader preferences, what worked, what did not, and why, and add findings about yourself as a reader to the *Reader analysis* activity below.

Activity: *Reader analysis*

This is a data-informed activity designed to capture the changes you need to make in an easy-to-follow format with clear action points.

✓ Use the data from the previous activity to create a list of actions for you to use when you're writing.

Note that this activity can be completed over time.

List what actions you can establish for yourself based on the preceding analysis. Leave plenty of space as you will possibly return to this as you move through the writing process.

It might begin to look something like this but will be more specific to you.

Reader analysis actions

- ✓ Reduce content, especially around the methodology; summarise and signpost instead of having a detailed justification.
- ✓ Reduce the number of subheadings but insert them more often in a shorter chapter to aid the reader in identifying the key sections they want to use. Rephrase your subheadings for reader ease of use.
- ✓ Signpost to other authors your reader can turn to for further information.
- ✓ Restructure.
- ✓ Can anything be removed? Is there a section that is perhaps better suited to an article? Is there a section you don't think is as successful?

- ✓ Write summary sections for each chapter so readers can skim for relevance.
- ✓ Make your writing accessible. This may include dispensing with language which justifies (e.g. I demonstrate that […]), avoid referring to previous chapter(s) in framing the next chapter and just repeating what you've already argued (e.g. as I showed in Chapter One […]), avoid jargon and provide a glossary of key terms.
- ✓ Reduce the number of footnotes, though this will likely follow by reducing the overall content; avoid using them to provide information not included in the body text.

Remember you are in the driving seat: you can choose what goes in and what does not!

Tip: Your writing evolves and develops with you. Think back to when you did not yet know how to write in an academic style, and now you have a PhD. It follows that your style will develop from postgraduate writer to book author. The journey, of course, will not stop there, unless you choose to stop writing.

Step 7. Choosing and approaching a publisher

Who do you want to publish with? You might already have a clear idea of publishers you want to approach, and that's great. If you're not yet sure, here are some approaches you can take:

i. Look back through your own bibliography to see if a particular publisher appears with a high frequency; if so, the chances are your work will fit with their profile.
ii. Go to individual publishers' websites and read about them. Do they publish books in your area? What impression do you get? What about the average costs of books by this publisher – are they similar to competitors?
iii. Ask colleagues for recommendations and then research them in more detail to see if you think they are the right fit for you and your book.

iv. Look at their Open Access policy: does it align with what you need? Open Access is discussed in more detail in Step 11.
v. Go with the publisher if it feels right, as they are likely a good fit for you and your work.

When it comes to approaching a publisher, there is no single route that you must follow. Their website may give you contact details for the editor in charge or ask you to fill out an online form. They will usually specify what information they need. It is a good idea to have a pitch ready about your book and why you want to publish with them.

You might also approach a publisher at a conference. Get chatting if you feel comfortable doing so. You could ask for a meeting in the near future to discuss your book proposal.

You might also try entering a book competition. Some publishers run competitions aimed at early career academics and PhD students nearing completion. The prize may be a book contract or a cash prize.

Step 8. Writing a proposal

When it comes to writing the proposal, take some time to learn about the form and style so you can pitch your book appropriately. Start by reading your intended publisher's style guide so that you shape your proposal to them from the start. You could also ask colleagues or potentially your supervisor if they would be willing to share a book proposal with you or if they would read a draft proposal and provide initial feedback.

Some publishers will provide you with peer review at the proposal stage while others provide peer review only when the full manuscript is ready. Your publisher will guide you step-by-step through the process.

You will need to be prepared to respond to the reviewer comments at whichever stage. How to respond is covered in depth in Step 27 of this book.

In your proposal, you will need to provide a level of detail about your book but also potential readership, as well as the practicalities, for example, if part of the material has already been published elsewhere and for which permissions will need to be obtained.

Requirements will vary, but it is advisable to spend some time working on:

- ✓ A summary of the book.
- ✓ The rationale for it – why this book, and why now.
- ✓ Detailed chapter synopses.
- ✓ A proposed table of contents.
- ✓ The estimated word count.
- ✓ Estimated numbers of images, tables or figures.
- ✓ A prospective submission date.
- ✓ Your potential readership and their reasons for buying your book.
- ✓ Any universities/institutions that may be likely to buy your book; you can give details such as the sorts of modules for which your book would be suitable. It is worth spending time looking at course modules at various institutions to show your market potential. This is useful later when it comes to marketing the book.
- ✓ Competing books – you need to show you know the market, their potential and their limitations.
- ✓ What makes your book unique compared to existing books on the market.
- ✓ People who can endorse your book (ask them for permission first).
- ✓ List any potential peer reviewers from your field; your publisher will decide whether or not to approach them.

You also need to send in one, or sometimes two, sample chapters to demonstrate your work, but remember it is just a sample. You can still change and improve it.

Step 9. Setting your submission deadline

Setting the deadline is something we usually get wrong. We underestimate how long we'll need, even with experience, because life intervenes. While we aim to meet the original deadline, it isn't always possible.

When I set my deadline, I just took a guess, based on when I wanted it to be done by, and estimated it would take just over a year. I was wrong. For some people it takes two years, for others more like three.

There are reasons, aside from inexperience, as to why we don't get the deadline right. Along with writing your book, you'll likely be applying for jobs, learning your new role(s), possibly moving for work and everything that that entails. Some, albeit by no means all, PhDs are placed under an embargo – either as a result of institutional policy or for specific reasons, not least around publications. Check your university requirements and factor any conditions into your decision on when to try and publish. Consider also the timeliness of the topic and whether it is time restricted. Any deadline is a best estimate, however.

To give you an approximate formula to work with, try out the activity on the next page. This should give you a deadline that takes into account how life intervenes, meaning you are less likely to need to delay. Remember the priority is not to publish quickly, but to publish well. There will be other mitigating factors to consider that are unique to you. Some topics are more time sensitive, for example. Whatever your individual circumstances, know that you are starting from a position of strength in that you have something to adapt into a book, rather than starting from scratch.

Activity: *Process for calculating your deadline*

This activity is designed to help you calculate with some degree of accuracy when you'll be able to submit your manuscript. Follow the steps.

List all your competing time commitments. Note how many hours this leaves you a week.

How many hours do you need to write a chapter? Base this on your experience to date.

Multiply the hours available by the hours needed to write a chapter. Then multiply that figure by the number of chapters.

Note – you may prefer writing at specific times rather than weekly, e.g. non-teaching weeks, but you need an approximate measure to work with for this calculation

Now add on an additional two months to factor in other things in your life – time away, moving, family commitments, illness, or injury.

Now you should have a realistic, workable timeframe.

This is only a best guess, based on your experience to date.

Step 10. Understanding publication processes

Depending on your publisher, you may receive a contract once your book proposal has been accepted, though some publishers only issue contracts once you submit your complete manuscript. The contracts should follow the industry standard, but you may find it reassuring to have someone more experienced look over the contract before signing.

You may understand your side of the book-writing process well, but how much do you understand from the publisher's side? Take a few minutes here to think about it.

Hint: Knowing nothing about it is a perfectly acceptable answer.

Frustration over the process can be common so setting expectations at this stage can be useful. Let's take a glance over what happens on the publisher's side, so you get a sense of timelines for making your book happen.

Throughout the process, your commissioning editor will keep in contact with you, checking on your progress. You will also receive administrative tasks to complete, including publicity material and cover designs for approval.

Your commissioning editor will put anonymous reviewers in place and, once you submit your manuscript, it will be sent out to them. While the publisher will agree a deadline for the return of the review, they are dependent on the reviewers' availability. Reviewers are sometimes offered a book voucher or even a small sum and, while reviewing is all part of the academic life, it is rarely the top priority, particularly at peak times in the academic year or during industrial action. This inevitably impacts on turnaround times.

Once reviews have been received your commissioning editor will send you the findings. We discuss how to deal with peer review later in Step 27.

Whilst your manuscript is under review, work on your book doesn't have to come to a halt: other jobs such as publicity forms can be completed.

Once you have submitted your revised draft you will then be sent preliminary proofs to check through and a second set of proofs following the implementation of amendments from the first. Turnaround times will vary but this end of the process is usually quicker, for example, one month between proofs.

Once the final proof has been signed off, the manuscript will go to print. Your publisher will give you an update on when to expect your author copies. While this process is happening you will collaborate with your publisher on promoting your book.

Step 11. Costing your publication

There are potential costs around publishing to be aware of at the outset, namely those associated with Open Access and in some instances with publication subsidies.

Let us consider Open Access first. You may already be familiar with it, especially if you've already published some of your work. Open Access does have potential benefits, particularly by making your work accessible to a wider audience. There are different types of Open Access, different costing structures and different requirements. As a starting point, turn to your institution's policies to see what requirements they stipulate. If your PhD was funded by an external research council, then also check their requirements for Open Access on books resulting from funded PhD research. Then reach out to specialists within your institution's library to ask for the latest guidance so you can make informed decisions.

Activity: *Should I publish Open Access?*

This is a planning activity designed to help you prepare for the administration around your book. Use the flowchart below to map out the stages you need to follow.

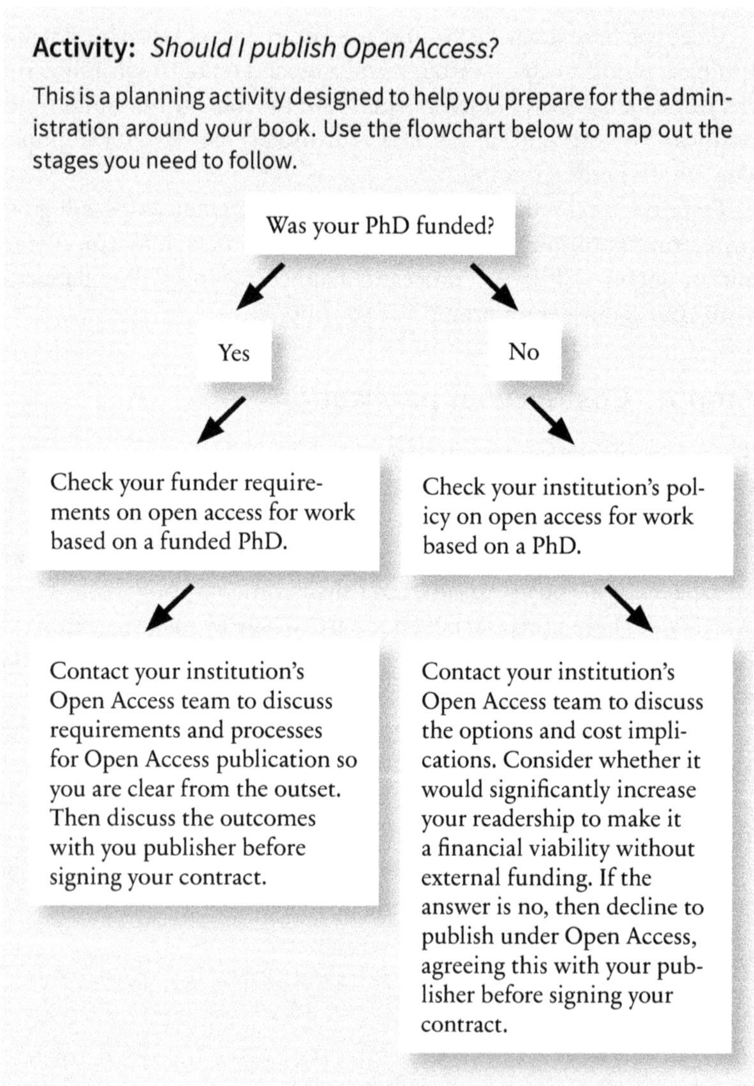

Publication subsidies are a feature of some, but no means all academic publishers. The subsidy will be determined by the length of the book and costs associated with any image usage. If you have a subsidy to pay, there are ways to try and cover the costs. It is worth devising a strategy, or better yet strategies, such as those on the next page.

Activity: *Funding strategising*

This is a planning activity designed to help you generate funding ideas in the event you have publication fees to cover. Read the strategies below and decide if they would work for you. If not, use them as a basis for your own and make a note of the strategies you decide upon.

- Save a specified amount per month in a separate account
- Research sources of funding at your institution and local or international bodies
- Approach subject associations about funding and apply near to completion (monies usually have to be spent in the financial year awarded)
- Approach employer(s) about using allocated research funds to offset costs

Step 12. Using images in your book

You may need to use images in your book. Ensure that the images are needed for reader understanding before selecting them. It will likely be your responsibility to obtain permission to use them. Check out how they are licensed. Images that are available via the internet under Creative Commons licencing are usually accompanied by usage information. If you are using archival images, the archive will provide usage information and contact details. It is advisable to start securing permission early in the process so that if you do need to pay for image usage you can factor this into the overall costs and have permission granted in good time so that it does not delay the publication process. You may of course wish to use your own photographs (e.g. of locations, architecture, sculpture), in which case copyright likely rests with you.

Activity: *Image permission tracker*

This activity is designed to help you ensure you have covered all necessities around image usage.

Populate the tracker document with information as you gather it.

Image to use	Image held by	Permission granted	Associated costs

Step 13. Obtaining permissions on previously published work

During your PhD, you may have already published one or more parts of your thesis that you nevertheless wish to integrate into your book. This is standard practice, and permissions are usually granted. Your publisher will ask about plans to use published work and will guide you through seeking permission. It is advisable to do this early in the process to avoid administrative delays in the publication.

Step 14. Providing translations

If your work includes quotations in another language, you'll need to provide a translation. If your work is solely in the one language, skip over to the next step.

When it comes to providing translations, if the works you want to cite are already available in translation, then citing the published versions will provide the most straightforward and swiftest option. If they aren't, however, you have two key options – you can engage a translator or translation agency, or you can translate for yourself. Let's look at the pros and cons of engaging a translator or translation agency.

	Pros	Cons
The translations should be to a high standard.	✓	
You do not hold copyright for the works.		✓
It potentially saves you time.	✓	
Translation is calculated on a per word basis, albeit with varying rates for repeated words. Can you afford it?		✓
Issue of who owns copyright of the translation.		✓
It is harder to translate small amounts of decontextualised text than longer pieces, precisely because the context which helps determine the style and other translation choices is absent.		✓

Given how well you know your work and your sources it is likely that you are best placed to translate for yourself, even if you are not confident in it. Try out the following activity using some of the excerpts you need to translate. Re-use it as many times as you like.

Activity: *Translation Generator*

This is a creative activity designed to help you practice, and boost your confidence in, translation, whilst simultaneously creating the content that you need.

i. Choose a short piece of text or quotation. Now consider what your priorities are for this translation, for example, should it have the narrator's voice; keep cultural references in the original language with the terms glossed for clarity?
ii. Next translate the passage freely. Then take another colour pen/change the font colour and annotate your translation with comments – what do you like, what does and doesn't work?
iii. Now translate the same passage again, this time doing a very literal translation, a word for word matching exercise. Again, take a different colour pen/change the font colour and annotate your translation with comments – what do you like, what does and doesn't work?

iv. Lay or view the translations side by side. Compare them and refer to your notes on your translation priorities. Ask yourself how well each translation fits with them and what changes do you want to make.
v. Now write a third version based on your analysis of the first two translations.
vi. When you have completed all your translations, ask a colleague or friend to look over them and do a sense check. If no one is available, leave your translations aside for now and look at them again after a little time has elapsed.

Step 15. Explaining what working on your book means

You might think you know what working on your book means, but if I asked you to explain in detail, as if to someone outside of academia, how would you explain it? I've included this question in response to the multiple conversations I've had on this topic with early career academics feeling conflicted about their various work and publication commitments, specifically the dominance of the former at the sake of the latter. The result is that they can feel plagued by anxiety or guilt around their work. These feelings need challenging. To do this we need to consider what constitutes working on a book. In fact, a more pertinent question might be this: Is writing a chapter **the only way** to be working on your book?

Activity: *Defining what you do*

This is an analytical activity designed to enable you to think about the whole process, attempting to combat potential sources of anxiety in the process.

Follow this flow chart and write out a rationale for your choices, this can be in prose or bullet point form. There is no correct answer.

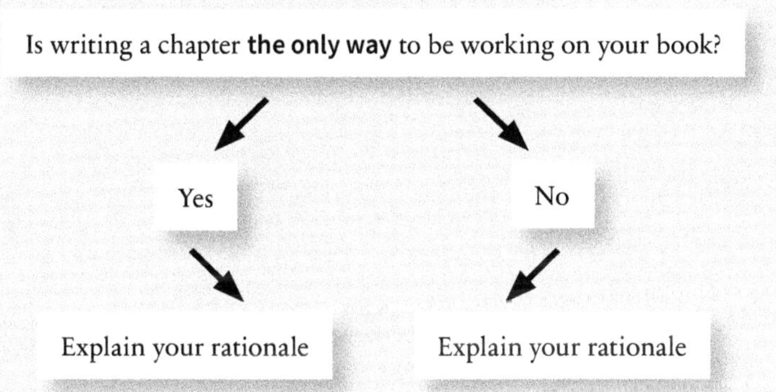

Write your rationale here:

Example rationale

My answer is no. Writing a chapter is the main part of working on the book, but it is not the only thing to do. Working on the book also includes:

- Thinking through sections (with or without making notes)
- Additional research to supplement the book and keep it as contemporaneous to the time of publication as possible
- Administrative tasks related to the book
- Engaging students and colleagues in the processes of choosing images for the book
- Presenting work-in-progress papers based on it
- Editing and revising drafts
- Searching and applying for funding
- Talking through your work – in seminars, presentations, writing retreats, public talks, podcasts

Breaking the process down into its component parts enables an understanding of the process. In addition, it is important for writer self-esteem and motivation at different points. This is particularly pertinent when you may feel as though you have little time to write. Instead of feeling conflicted you realise you can still be working on your monograph even if you're not writing. This relieves some of the pressure so that when you do sit down to write again you feel more motivated and encouraged.

Step 16. Identifying obstacles and how to swerve them

Throughout the process of writing, you will likely encounter an array of obstacles. The activity in this section is designed to help you identify them and then swerve them. Before we start, I'd like to suggest that although we may see them as obstacles, we don't need to see them as wholly negative. They can be exasperating or even overwhelming, but we can flip that reaction and see when and how they can also be constructive. The purpose of the following activity is to get you to see how what at first seems a hindrance can be seen or used differently, more constructively, and positively, which in turn helps your motivation and challenges negative feelings around writing.

Activity: *Sticking it out*

This is a creative activity that can be done individually but also lends itself to working with others to generate ideas, perspectives, as well as harnessing different experiences. For this activity you'll need a space to work in – you're going to need either an empty table or a wall space so you can move sticky notes/small pieces of paper around.

i. Take a sticky note/small piece of paper and write down one obstacle you have either come across already or anticipate you will encounter. Note that these may be academic obstacles, but they can also be everyday obstacles. The combination will be unique to you. There is no limit. Repeat the process until you feel you've listed everything you can think of.
ii. Now categorise them into obstacle types. Using either a sticky note or small piece of paper, write the following category headings, one per note: **practical, financial, psychological, other**.
iii. Place these category headings around your workspace. Make sure there is space around each category heading.
iv. Now place each obstacle around the most suitable heading; you may find an obstacle fits into more than one category, so go with the best fit.
v. Now take a different colour of sticky note/piece of paper, one per obstacle, and try to think of a solution or at least a suggestion of what to do in each scenario. You might think of multiple solutions, so list them all.
vi. Once you've finished, you'll see you've created guidance for yourself throughout the process. You might want to keep the notes as they are or stick them on a larger piece of paper. You might prefer to photograph it and keep it so that as you encounter an obstacle you only need to refer to your own guidance on how to swerve it.

Here are some examples of obstacles and how to swerve them:

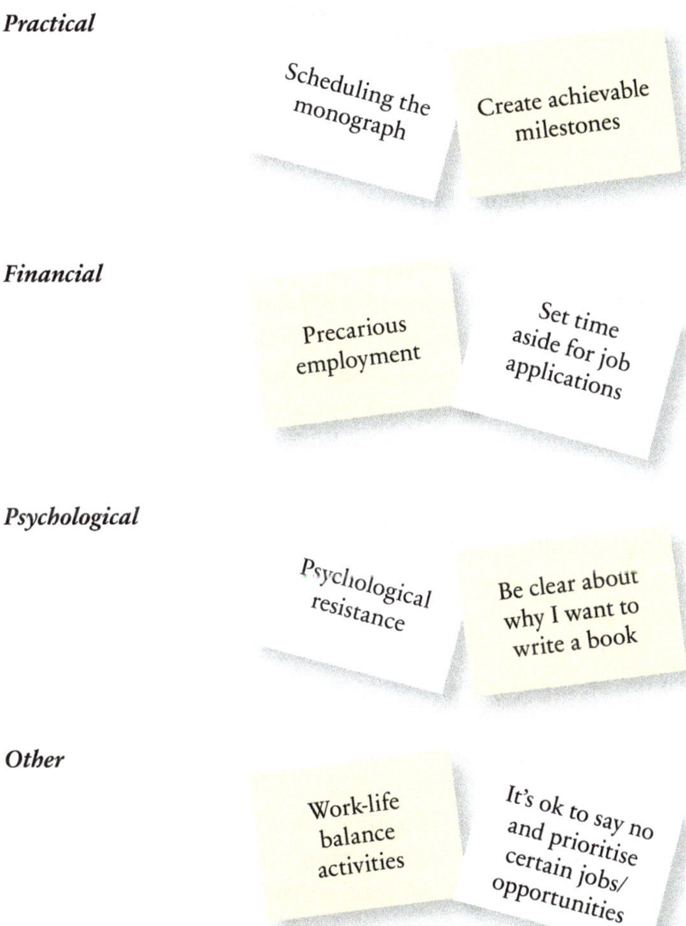

The above are only suggestions. You might find you have other solutions that work for you. Of course, more obstacles and solutions may present themselves as you work your way through the writing process, so you can keep building your own guidance.

Step 17. Competing demands and how to make use of them

> I'm still not entirely sure how I'll juggle other commitments alongside developing a book.
>
> [SW]

It is easy to succumb to time pressure and feel you have to get on with your book **now**. If you are feeling this, then **STOP.** Let me explain why you feel that pressure and then explain how and why time is your friend.

Partly, if not the main reason, we can feel pressured into getting on with the book as soon as possible post-viva is the need to secure a stable job, coupled with the belief that having a book will help us attain that. It may, or it may not. Securing a job – academic or non-academic – is dependent on multiple factors beyond both the book, and our control.

Let's assume in this example you are pursuing an academic pathway. Those factors include the Higher Education market, generally, and in your field, specifically, as well as job location, and whether you are able and willing to move for work. Contract type may also be a factor. If you are working in the UK market and you are on a teaching and scholarship or teaching-only contract, then research outputs, certainly REF eligible ones, are unlikely to count. Indeed, unless you are on a research contract, or teaching and research one, then you will have little or no time factored into your workload for writing up your research as it is not always a requirement. Research effectively becomes something you do in your own time. So, as tempting as it is to link publishing your book with getting a secure job – just **stop** a moment and think about it. If you equate the two and then you either cannot get on with your book **AND/OR** any job, permanent or temporary, does not materialise, then you're setting yourself up for a lot of psychological pressure.

If you rush a book and it reads like a PhD thesis, that's not going to help your career development. Finishing a PhD is a major undertaking. Just think about how mentally and physically tired you are from it. Are you really ready to write it, or at least write it quickly? If you create too much pressure on yourself, you may end up prolonging the process as writer's block sets in. Fast writing does not necessarily equate to good writing in either the immediate or longer term. If you write a book that reads like a PhD, who will read not just it, but also your next book? By accepting that writing it is a marathon not a sprint, you take the pressure off yourself. It helps you to have a feeling of control over the time you take on your book. I suggest you write it because you want to and write it when the time feels right to you and for you.

Once you see time as a friend, the question then becomes how to make use of the competing demands on your time, and to see how they can be made use of in writing your book. The following case study lists some of the competing demands on an average humanities-based early career academic's time when turning their PhD into a book and extrapolates from there to the ways they could also benefit their writing process directly and indirectly.

What you may notice immediately is that none of these directly look as if they help with writing – in fact, several look like hindrances – and to some extent they are, but there are also positives to be found. Look at the examples and apply them to your own circumstances.

Early career academic case study

	Negative Impact	**Constructive Interpretation**
Job hunting	Massive amounts of time taken up Huge source of frustration	✓ Relish writing time ✓ Use frustration as a motivator ✓ Make new connections/ network
New job(s)	Time taken learning new job, getting to know colleagues and students Little to no writing time	✓ Building skills in job, brings confidence that filters down into writing ✓ Time doing other things is also thinking time for the book after some distance from it
Moving homes	Time consuming Anxiety inducing Disorientating Tedious	✓ Reassurance of engaging with something familiar when everything else is new

	Negative Impact	Constructive Interpretation
Teaching, marking, admin	Time-consuming, especially if new to teaching Teaching new material Learning admin processes	✓ Observing how students learn and engage with materials – helps to get to know one of your target audiences, tailoring the book in turn ✓ Learning to block time for tasks ✓ Learning to set realistic, achievable goals

So, think about the competing demands on your time, and see if you too can find the positives to be gained. This helps to minimise frustration and a sense of not making progress when you cannot get to the book, and realise how other factors can help indirectly, too.

Step 18. Choosing other projects: when and why to (not) do them

Can or should you take on other projects when turning your PhD into a book? In some ways this is more than a simple binary question. It may be beyond your control through your job. Others may be projects of your own choosing. If it is the latter, the when is down to you. If it is the former, then you might not have a choice over the timing, but you do have control over how you benefit from it, be it learning something new, gaining experience of project management and, with it, possibly examples of good practice you can apply to your own work or, conversely, ways of working you would not seek to replicate.

Activity: *New project toolkits*

This is a reflective activity designed to enable you to make informed decisions about new projects whilst writing your book.

i. Complete Toolkits 1 and 2
ii. Compare your answers. Does one stand out as to why you should, or you shouldn't? Once you've compared your responses you can make an informed decision.

Toolkit 1

Reasons to take on a new project:

- It interests me ☐
- I need to do something different for a while ☐
- It links to my book in some way ☐
- It helps my career development ☐
- It helps me develop new knowledge ☐
- It helps me to decide whether to do my book ☐
- It helps me network ☐
- It only takes up a small amount of my time ☐

Your own reflections/additional reasons

Toolkit 2

Reasons not to take on a new project:

- I feel obligated ☐
- I do not have enough time ☐
- It is too different a topic ☐
- It is the wrong time ☐
- It won't help my career development ☐
- It will distract me from my book ☐
- It will only benefit others' research/REF outputs ☐

Your own reflections/additional reasons

Step 19. Keeping a log

When you already have a book to write, suggesting you write something else alongside it may seem just too much, not to mention a distraction from the very thing you are trying to do. Pause here for a second. Writing can seem like an overwhelming task. It is easy to feel as if you can't do it, and the book just doesn't get written. This isn't just common to first-time or academic authors but to all who write.

Now imagine how much more doable writing the book seems if you break it down into tasks. That alone may not be enough. Whilst you may know what you have got to do, motivating yourself to do it is also an essential part of the writing process. By keeping a log, you are able to chart how far down that road you have already travelled. You can keep a digital log, but sometimes something physical and tangible does the trick. If you keep your log in a small notebook, you can just add to it anytime, anywhere. This helps to chart your progress, and can be both comforting and motivational, especially after periods where you've not been able to write. This log can be a simple list of tasks completed, a word count per writing session; it can be a reflective log, noting your thoughts and feelings; or it can be a combination of any of these things and more.

Step 20. Getting back into the book

> It can be really tempting to wait until you have a free day before sitting down to write. But then, either the free day never comes or when it does, the pressure to be productive can be overwhelming.
>
> [CP]

A good book takes time to write. Invariably you will not be able to work exclusively on it. In fact, there will be times you just are not able to get on with it, which has nothing to do with motivation, and everything to do with juggling work, life and writing commitments. Whether the hiatus between the last section you wrote and the next thing you write is long or short, getting back into the book can be challenging. Having strategies to hand helps get you back into writing.

Activity: *Circle the writing strategy*

This motivational activity is designed to help you get back into writing after periods away from your book. The intention is to use it as an ongoing resource over the course of your writing. Descriptions are provided with each strategy, and you can use them more than once. Circle your chosen strategy and complete the suggested activity.

Diary Time 	*Block time in your diary that works for you and treat it as a meeting you must attend. It can be for a short time – just showing up helps you feel in control.*	**Time off** 	*Take time off. It is professional to do so. Time off is also essential for health and wellbeing, which in turn impacts on your writing.*
Customise your writing space 	*Make yourself a space in which to work – if something doesn't feel right – change it, no matter how small.*	**Plan 1 thing for your next writing session** 	*Plan just one thing that you will do next in your writing, where you will pick up from. It'll give you a sense of progression and make you feel in control.*
Write an abstract 	*Write an abstract for the section you are working on, identify your focus, key questions, key arguments, and conclusion.*	**Stick at it for 20 min** 	*Sometimes you don't want to write but stick with it for a short while. It is amazing how much just doing a just little helps when your motivation is flagging, or you are time poor.*
Small tasks list 	*Create a list of tasks to do so that even if you aren't able to write, you are making progress. It could include creating a contact list, looking for images to use, editing.*	**Use paper and pencil** 	*Go back to basics – pen or pencil and paper – just start writing, drawing, doodling – it can be incredibly restorative.*
Write with others 	*Write with others if you can – be it in a virtual space, physically in the same place or even remotely – texting with updates on progress.*	**Get and give feedback** 	*Ask someone you trust to read a short piece of your work and give you feedback – others' enthusiasm can be motivating. Return the favour – reading others' writing can be equally inspiring to get back into your own.*
Stop writing mid-sentence 	*Stop writing mid-sentence. This might sound counter-intuitive, but it can be motivating, creating the urge to write. It has the added benefit of easing you back in.*	**Take scissors to your writing** 	*Print a chapter, then take a pair of scissors to it. There's a satisfaction to it. This helps to free you to make changes, disregard something if it doesn't work more than just looking at words on a screen.*

Step 21. Identifying the value of involving others

No book is ever the work of one person alone. You know this already. You wrote your PhD with the support of others, for example, supervisors, examiners, peers. Writing your book is no different in this sense – it will inevitably involve other people, for example, publishers, editors, reviewers. In another sense there is a change to get used to. You no longer have formal supervision, even if your supervisors are involved informally.

> The prospect of writing a book without the same level of support as I had for my PhD is definitely an intimidating prospect. I think it is important to remember that there are still plenty of ways to gain peer support and feedback. Within academia we are quite lucky that mentorship is valued highly and once you establish these types of connections in a respectful and mutually fulfilling way, people are often very willing to give you some support.
>
> [SW]

In addition, there can be value in involving other people, for example, colleagues and students, and doing so for practical as well as motivational reasons. The benefits of this can include opportunities for informal and formal feedback at different stages of the process. You can also encourage others in sharing your ongoing work. This can be especially pertinent if you have students with whom you share your work. It gives them an insight into it and processes, but also into academia more generally. In turn this can incentivise you to write, help combat feelings of isolation that can come with writing and help build positive staff–student relationships. There is no need to anticipate every involvement at the outset – opportunities will emerge at different points in time if you are open to them. When either an opportunity arises or you have a specific need for involving others in the process, be strategic in your actions in order to get the most from it.

Activity: *Deciding on aims and activities for involving others*

This is a knowledge-building activity designed to help you generate opportunities to enrich your book writing at different stages in the process. This activity foregrounds aims and links them to practical activities. It is designed to act as a model, helping you generate your own aims and activities as suited to your own book.

i. Read through the aims and activities below
ii. Think of two aims and associated activities linked to your own book and put them into practice

Aim To test out how accessible your writing is to your intended reader.

Activity Ask target readers, e.g. students to read a chapter and give them a feed-back sheet to complete, or even a quick quiz to see how they have understood your work, and what else you might need to do to make it accessible.

Aim To decide which images to include in your monograph.

Activity Curate a temporary exhibition – physical or virtual – inviting passersby to vote on the images. Set out a clear explanation of the exhibition's purpose and state how many images can be voted for. You then have collatable data to inform your choices whilst generating interest in your book.

Aim To build networks of colleagues & potential readers.

Activity Present at a conference, a workshop, a work-in-progress session, to a community group, as a guest speaker on a podcast.

Aim To get feedback on a chapter or complete manuscript.

Activity Ask a colleague or colleagues to read a chapter for you. Offer to do the same for them, not just so that it is quid pro quo but we can always also learn from reading others' work.

Aim ______________________________

Activity ______________________________

____

____

____

Aim ______________________________

Activity ______________________________

____

____

____

Step 22. Gauging the size of your bibliography

The bibliography that accompanied your PhD is likely to be substantial. In your book it needs to be substantial enough for credibility, but not so extensive that it gives your book the feel of a document to be assessed and marked. It is also worth noting that bibliographies take time to compile, and usually longer than anticipated. There is no exact figure of how many entries you should have, but a little over half of the PhD version is a good guideline. My PhD bibliography had 460 entries in total and my book had 270. So how do you decide?

Activity: *Compiling your bibliography*

This activity is designed to facilitate the process of compiling your bibliography. You will need a copy of your manuscript and a fresh copy of your PhD bibliography in either digital or print form. Ideally you will do this once you have a first draft of your manuscript.

i. Check every reference in your manuscript against the PhD bibliography. Everything you've cited needs including. Put a tick √ against each entry that appears in both.
ii. Refer back to your reader analysis in Step 6. Think of your readers as you read through the remaining entries. Consider whether they may find them useful. If the answer is yes, put a tick against the entry. If not, then strike it through.
iii. Next, open up a digital copy of your PhD bibliography, creating a duplicate version so you don't inadvertently lose the original. Using the duplicate copy delete all the unnecessary entries you have identified.
iv. Now add in any additional entries of new works you've read since.

Note: Your publisher will have their own bibliography style guide, and this may differ from your previous style, so work through your bibliography until all entries are consistent with the style guide and then merge the document with your manuscript.

Step 23. Writing the acknowledgements

Writing acknowledgements can be tricky, not because of the form, but owing to the politics of who to acknowledge and for what. There are some accepted conventions. With a book based on your PhD, it is customary to acknowledge your former supervisors. You should, of course, also acknowledge your publisher and editorial team. If you received any financial support towards your publication subsidy, then this must also be acknowledged; it is usually a condition of the funding. It can feel as if you need to acknowledge many people, and this is the part that can feel political – do I mention X, will I offend Y if I don't? The simple answer is no, you don't have to. It is up to you to decide who to include.

Activity: Acknowledgements template

This activity is designed to help organise your content.

i. Use the template and input data in the relevant sections, then put it aside for several days.
ii. Look again at the populated template and reflect on whether each individual should be there. A few days' reflection may lead you to reconsider whether someone really helped you. Cross off anyone you are uncertain about.
iii. Write up the acknowledgements in narrative form using at least one paragraph per section.

Supervisor(s)
Publisher and editorial team
Any financial support given (Name the individual/organisation but not the amount)
Groups, e.g. students, friends, family (1–3 paragraphs, outlining what support, e.g. students' enthusiasm, family support, etc.)
Individuals, usually colleagues, who have made a substantial contribution – list them alphabetically by surname

Step 24. Editing

Editing tends to be understood as a task that comes after writing. To an extent, I agree, but I would also argue that it is a multi-stage process that begins during the writing process. It will be a large task, but it can be made more manageable by editing at multiple stages, and with an emphasis on different focal points with each edit. Let me explain what I mean by breaking it down into stages, before giving you some general tips.

a. Edit as you write.

Writing and editing are distinct tasks. You should avoid editing immediately after writing, as you're too close to the text to spot any significant issues, be they conceptual or grammatical. However, there is nothing to say you cannot take an edit-as-you-write approach. As you sit down to continue with the chapter you are currently working on, start by editing. Arguably this can be beneficial, not only in making the later final edit easier but as a means of getting back into the flow of writing, re-engaging with the ideas, and finding your authorial voice again. Focus on the ideas, the concepts at this stage, considering whether they have been clearly conveyed. You might spot grammatical and or typographical errors at this stage, and it is fine to correct them as you go, but your primary focus is on ensuring the ideas are tight and the content has a logical flow. Once you've completed this, continue writing, then repeat the process the next time you work on the chapter.

b. Edit before beginning the next chapter.

When you've finished a chapter, as tempting as it may be to move on immediately, set it aside. If you can, leave it at least a week before you look at it again, so that you can come to it fresh. If you've edited along the way, then you can focus on the grammatical, the typographical as well as the formatting and style of your chapter. You can do this over several sittings rather than all at once, or at the very least take breaks from it to keep your focus fresh and your mind alert to the task. You may also find it easier to work from a physical copy rather than a digital one or vice versa. Printed and on-screen versions offer two different ways of viewing and reviewing your work; both are valid, though you may find a preference for one medium over another. Either way you can also adopt any of the following to aid the process:

- Print on a different coloured paper/change the background colour on a digital version – this helps errors to stand out that you may otherwise overlook as you see what you expect to rather than what you need to.

- Alternatively change the font colour – again this helps to alert you to errors.
- Use different pens/colours to mark-up different error types.

What you will need to help with the process:

- A note of any common errors you know you tend to make, for example, certain spellings, comma usage.
- Your publisher's style guide (if you are editing digitally, it is easier to have this as a printout or on a separate screen so you can compare it to your document, rather than switching back and forth between tabs).

Whether you print or use a digital version, here's a step-by-step process you can adopt wholesale or adapt to your own needs and follow.

- Read through the completed chapter, looking for any error that immediately springs to mind. You may also find it helpful to read it in reverse. This takes a little time but is valuable for revealing errors, as they become more apparent when the expected format is altered.
- Read the chapter again, this time focusing on each line in turn. Have any notes to hand on your common errors and check for them. Mark-up the text/document where you need to make changes.
- Now use the publisher's style guide and check you have been consistent. Check one style point at a time, for example, citation and referencing format usage, format for quotes, use of italicisation for foreign words, paragraph indentation.

Once you are satisfied you have covered everything, implement the changes on the digital version, checking off each amendment as you go. When finished, put the chapter aside and move onto the next, repeating the editing process with that chapter.

c. Edit your manuscript before submission.

If you've followed the process above with each chapter, your task once you get a complete manuscript should be a little easier. It still takes time, and I'd recommend taking breaks or completing the task in more than one sitting, but by this point you should have a relatively carefully checked document. However, that is not to suggest it is entirely error free or that errors couldn't have been introduced in merging individual chapters into one document. So, repeat the preceding steps, looking out for consistency in style, especially around headings and subheadings. Check that references are correctly numbered. Once you are happy with any amendments, you're ready to submit.

There is, of course, software available to help you check your work, such as grammar and spelling checkers. You could also try using an immersive reader. Switching modes can be useful when checking a text, as you may pick up on something through listening rather than reading alone for example. Do make use of software but think carefully before you implement an amendment. Writing is, after all, a cognitive process. By all means use such embedded software, but make all final decisions for yourself.

You may be considering using AI to help with writing or editing your book. A word of caution here. Check with your publisher beforehand as they will likely want you to disclose if you have used AI at any stage in the process. Remember that generative AI is merely providing probabilistic output and does not possess the knowledge that you do about your subject. We each have our own unique authorial voice that no software can fully emulate, nor would you want software to stilt it.

It is also worth noting that this won't be the last time you check your work. As your submitted manuscript moves its way through the publishing process, it will be checked by your publisher and sent back with mark-ups for you to address, so do your best but remember yours won't be the only eyes on it before it reaches its readers.

Step 25. Submitting your draft and what follows

Once you are ready with your draft manuscript, send it to your publisher, usually via email, unless your publisher stipulates otherwise. Submitting can make you feel many different things – it can be anti-climactic, it can be exciting or nerve wracking, and it can also feel like a huge relief.

All emotional responses are equally valid. However you feel about it, treat yourself to some time to do something else entirely, to celebrate this milestone, or just take time just to pause. An array of tasks will soon follow, so rest and recharge, so you are ready for them. Let's start with the topic of publicity.

You will likely be asked by your publisher to assist with information for publicising your book. You may find the work you did on your proposal useful once again here. The purpose of these forms is to give your book the widest possible reach upon publication. You could discuss with your editor about potential journals to approach that might be interested in reviewing your book.

You will also be asked to write a publicity text. These are always short, around 200 words, which can make writing them tricky, given the volume of things you could say. Think of your reader again here, as you did in Step 6, and write for them. Write a few versions of your publicity text, and ask a few colleagues to look at them, and see what appeals. You can also look at publicity texts around recently published works in your field and again analyse them for what works.

Tip: Task one is to hook your reader in. They've picked up your book, or clicked on the cover online, and now you want them to choose it. Open with a statement or claim. Then proceed to explaining what your book focuses on, how, and what it offers the reader. Lastly add one or two overarching conclusions.

Step 26. Handling peer review

> I was anxious about getting peer review back. It felt as though I might fail. In the end it was really useful. I came to realise that my anxiety was linked to my own lack of self-confidence, to my imposter syndrome. Once I actually had my peer review that feeling went away.
>
> [HP]

Peer review is an essential part of every publication process, even if we find it uncomfortable at times. That is hardly surprising given the amount of time and energy, including emotional investment that goes into writing anything. Also, your response to it may well be refracted through previous experiences – if you have had negative experiences, perhaps a difficult PhD – all of these factors feed into how you feel and may impact on how you respond to peer review. Being anxious about peer review, or sensitive to comments is not an indication of the quality of your work, but it is worth reflecting on why you might feel that way, especially before responding to reviewer comments. Imagine if you published without it and someone then pointed out how you could argue something more succinctly; you'd probably wish someone had said something earlier.

Remember, though, that the aim of peer review should be to ensure rigour and quality. You may find it reassuring to know that there are codes of conduct for peer reviewing, and your publisher will usually provide their reviewers with best practice guidelines.

There are many myths around peer review, and not all peer reviews are equal. The confessions of a peer reviewer letter in this section, will, I hope, dispel at least some of them. In the best-case scenario, the reader's reports will be intellectually stimulating, enabling you to re-engage with your work with a freshness and a keen eye for sharpening it. It is worth remembering that you can reject some peer review suggestions, especially if you feel they are not appropriate, so long as a courteous explanation is provided in response. Similarly, a suggestion may not work in your view, but it may provoke your thinking which means you can take the suggestion in a different direction that augments your work, just differently from the way the reviewer suggested. Whatever the feedback, it helps though to understand the peer review process, and after that, strategies for how to handle it.

Once you submit, your commissioning editor will pass your work on to selected peer reviewers in your field, who should remain anonymous to you, though they should declare any conflict of interest to the publisher if any exists. Peer review can vary from anything from a number of small recommendations, to a revise and resubmit, as well as rejection, though your publisher has the ultimate say. The reviewer gives recommendations only.

When you receive the reviews, always make sure to acknowledge receipt and advise that you'll be back in touch when you've had time to consider the comments. No matter what review you've received, the contents take time to digest. Go through each comment and decide:

a) are you clear on what they are recommending, b) do you agree with the comments, c) what actions, if any, will you now take. It is perfectly acceptable to ask questions of the reviewers' comments, even if this means your commissioning editor goes back to the reviewer for further clarification.

You can then decide on your strategies. Use the reviewer comments as a checklist, ticking off points as you go. As you make any recommended changes, note them down against the comment, perhaps in a different colour, so you can demonstrate what amendments you have made and how you have engaged with the reviewer comments.

> When the email with the peer reviews attached comes through, I always want to click on it immediately and find out what these anonymous people thought – did they love my work?! However, it's usually best to pause. I ask myself: do I need to open this right now? Sometimes it's good to wait a while until I have the energy and the emotional space to deal with the reviews.
>
> [CP]

Activity: *Preparing hypothetical strategies*

This is a knowledge-building activity designed to give you some tools and ideas as to how to deal with peer review effectively. It uses real-world scenarios to which you will create hypothetical strategies. These might differ from the reviewer feedback you receive, but this activity affords you a practice run so you can then apply this approach to your work in due course.

i. Read each strategy in turn, jotting down ideas as to how you could respond in that scenario.
ii. Now read the suggested strategy and annotate it with your own ideas.
iii. Using these scenarios as a guide, create two of your own.
iv. Write two responses to the scenarios you created. The first is an emotional reaction, writing it out of your system. This is the version you would never send but it is a cathartic exercise. Then write a second, measured response. This is the strategy you would adopt.

Note: This activity can be done individually or discursively amongst a group of peers.

Scenario 1

The reviewers were largely positive but pointed out a number of typographical and punctuation errors. I didn't spot these on the first edit. How will I make sure to address them now?

Write your initial thoughts here

Suggested Strategy 1

Look at the type of error highlighted, then look up the grammatical rule. Can you see how the error has occurred? If yes, go through the manuscript and highlight each instance of the error, then amend. Rather than solely relying on yourself, ask a colleague or colleagues to read through as a favour and you'll do them a favour in return. In the best-case scenario, you have enough willing colleagues as you do chapters, then you get multiple sets of eyes on your work checking it for you. Discuss turnaround times with your publisher so you can get the work completed in a reasonable timeframe that is neither too brief so that you feel pressured, nor too long that it extends the process unnecessarily.

Scenario 2

The reviewers made several suggestions on refining some sections, but their recommendations are ambiguous and I'm not clear on what is expected. How will I ensure I engage with the comments to the satisfaction of my publisher?

Write your initial thoughts here

Suggested Strategy 2

Take a look at their comments – do you have an inkling as to what they mean, or none at all? Whether you have some idea or none, go back to your editor and ask for clarity, explaining you are unclear but that you want to ensure you fully engage with the reviewer comments. This usually will help you secure sufficient clarity for you to be able to work on the comments. Agree a reasonable timeframe with your publisher in which to do this.

Scenario 3

The reviewers have indicated that my book reads like a PhD and have suggested a revise and resubmit, and that I engage with a number of additional works. I wasn't expecting this. I don't know what to do.

Write your initial thoughts here

Suggested Strategy 3

This is quite a common scenario. You might not believe it initially, but a much stronger book can emerge as a result. Remember the aim is to publish well rather than to publish quickly. Firstly, set time aside to work through the comments, Do you notice themes emerging? Grouping the comments can help you decide what to address first. Then try going back to earlier sections of this book, using the exercises to help you in rethinking and reshaping. After that plan in some time to consider the reviewers' suggestions and whether they might work. You won't really know until you try. Once you have, you'll be in a better position to respond to the reviewers' comments for your publisher, then have a conversation with your commissioning editor and agree on the next steps.

Your scenarios

Write your own scenario here

Write an emotional reaction here

Write a measured response here

Write your own scenario here

Write an emotional reaction here

Write a measured response here

If any, or all, of those scenarios were off-putting, the following activity should help humanise the peer review process. It aims to take the anxiety out of peer review by putting you in the reviewer's position. One day that will be you. Seeing the process from their perspective gives you a greater overall understanding of the purpose and aims, enabling you to better deal with peer review when it arrives.

Activity: *Getting to know a peer reviewer*

This is a reflective activity in three stages. Follow the instructions below.

i. Take a few minutes to think about the peer review process, then list everything you can think of including commonly held perceptions, together with any concerns or fears you may have. Leave space around the list so you can annotate it later.
ii. Now read confessions of a peer reviewer.
iii. Look back at your list. Is there anything you would change? If so, annotate it. Note down how you feel about peer review now.

Write your thoughts and perceptions on the peer review process here

Confessions of a peer reviewer

I get it, the mention of peer review can make your blood run cold. I'm a peer reviewer and even I'm uncomfortable when I first get reviews back on my work. Deep down I always want to know that my work is good enough, hence my heightened emotional response. It doesn't help when you come across the infamous reviewer 2. We've all been there, and it isn't a pretty place. I've had work rejected and it still hurts, not least because it feels unfair. However, that doesn't mean they are necessarily wrong about the quality of my work at that point. Nor does it mean because I've felt that rejection that I'm going to wave everything through automatically. Peer review should always be given with care, consideration, constructive and informed criticism that is linked to clear guidance and action points. Now you and I both know that not every reviewer would be like this, I may be unique, but this style should be the aspiration. I try to be the type of reviewer that I would like to be reviewed by, however idealistic that may be. I want to do my best for the author, whether they're a long-established writer or new to the field, so that their book can be the best it possibly can be. I can only speak for myself in this and heartily encourage you to do the same when your time to do peer review comes. So, this is my little request to you – I'm about – I hope – to demystify the process, and in return all I ask is that when your time comes to peer review, you too try and set a similar standard, a sort of quid pro quo arrangement between you and I.

I guess one thing to note is that a good review takes time – and yes, academics are always short of time, but I do the best I can. Reviewers should always be remunerated even if it is through vouchers to spend with that publisher, rather than a fee. If I'm ever asked to review for free, I always decline, as I don't agree with a business model that asks for free labour, nor do I think they'll serve the author's best interests.

Anyway, getting to the process itself. When I sit down with a manuscript, the very first thing I do is fire up my computer and do some cursory research. If the manuscript is for a first book based on a PhD thesis, I look for it and begin a comparison. I expect similarity, of course. However, there should be differences, developments. I understand the pressure to publish, but I also know how a rushed book is not going to help your career development. If your manuscript reads as though the author has gone through their PhD using the advanced search function and replaced 'thesis' or 'dissertation' with 'book' or 'monograph' and only a few other changes, then I'll already be inclined to advise a revise and resubmit, even before I have read very closely. Ditto if the word counts barely differ. I'm not only thinking about the author at this point, when I review, I'm also thinking about the reader.

[cont'd]

If I note, 'this reads like a PhD thesis', I'm not trying to actively hinder your publication pathway, I'm trying to help you. I'm thinking about your credibility; if you haven't guessed so already, a quick rehash of your PhD thesis won't help you gain it. Ask yourself this, do you want to publish a book, or do you want to publish a book that people will read?

Most of the works I get to review, I do recommend for publication – I'm always looking to do that, and it saddens me if I do suggest revise and resubmit because I know it's going to be an unpleasant experience for the author. I do also take the time to give considered suggestions. I hope that if I give them, you'll follow up on them. I've not made recommendations for the sake of making them, but because I've seen something in your work that connects to something else and therefore adds to your work. If I've noted something is not clear or an argument under-developed, I'll be suggesting how you can improve it.

I know my recommendations are just that – recommendations. I've done reviews in the past where none of my recommendations have been implemented and the work has been published pretty much as I saw it at review stage. That's the author and publisher's purview.

I'm a peer reviewer. I am not your enemy. I am your critical friend. I sincerely hope this helps you as you work on your monograph.

Step 27. Proofreading and indexing

Once your manuscript has been revised and approved, the copy-editing and typesetting process begins. At this point, it will only be errors, inaccuracies or inconsistencies that you can mark up for correction. You will likely receive two rounds of formatted proofs to check, and the production team at your publisher will guide you through this process.

Indexing is an essential part of your book. It will likely be completed once the formatted page proofs are available with the final page numbers. You can assess the key terms and names that you want to highlight, and identify the page numbers where they appear. You can have professional indexers take on the task, but there are three factors to consider here:

i. The cost of paying for a professional to compile the index for you. Can you afford it, and is it worth it?

ii. Who is best placed to know what to include? The answer to that is YOU! It is your book, you know it in detail, so you already have an instinct for most, if not all, the entries that will make it into the final version.

iii. Compiling your own index also helps ensure consistency, for example, in spelling of names.

The question to ask here is not how, but why to index? To answer this, think back to your intended audiences. If you think that your average reader is less likely to read your book from cover to cover and more likely to dip in and out, then it becomes apparent that they'll need to home in on key parts of it. For that, the index is an essential tool. Your reader may skim through the index first to see if there is anything of use to them and, if not, likely reject it. So, you want the index to be a handy guide to your book – which begs the question, how do you know what to include and exclude from your index?

To answer the 'how' and 'what' questions, look back at Step 6. This is your springboard. From this you will first be able to list key umbrella themes or headings. These will vary from book to book but to give you an idea they might be:

- People (theorists, historians, filmmakers, politicians)
- Historical figures/groups
- Places
- Acronyms (including variants, and translated terms used)
- Key concepts and terms (including variants, and translated terms used)
- Key debates
- Key events

Activity: *Compiling the index*

This is a practical activity with a creative element designed to minimise input errors and make data manageable.

i. Write down each theme or heading on a separate sticky note or scrap of paper.

ii. Choose one theme and add all the items that fall under that theme. Don't worry about the order or duplication across themes at this stage.
iii. Create a new document and begin inputting your data, this time in alphabetical order, physically ticking each paper entry off as you go. At this stage you will identify any duplication.
iv. Now skim read your formatted proof pages finding each item, noting the page numbers, aligning them with the entries in your index. You can either use a physical copy or a digital version, using the control and find function to locate the items, ensuring you have all the possible page numbers.
v. Check your completed index against the publisher's index guide to ensure consistency of style. Each publisher has their own guide where they set out their style requirements, beyond the fact that entries need to be listed alphabetically and accompanying page references in numerically ascending order. These may include rules on order of entries and sub-entries by grammar function, for example, noun first, or rules on italicisation of foreign terms.

You can do this on paper or digitally, whichever you prefer. Do note that your index usually has to be submitted as word document, but you may find it helpful to create a spreadsheet for collating and organising all your data.

You don't have to do the indexing in one sitting; indeed, I'd suggest you don't, as it is a task that requires intense concentration so is perhaps best done in short bursts. By focusing on themes or headings it is easier to get back into after a break in the task.

Once you've done all of the above, and checked it through, your index is done. The question that needs to be asked about all of the above, though, is how many entries should there be? There is no precise figure, as each book is unique, but to give you a rough estimate to work to, use the number breakdown on the next page as an approximate guideline.

Total wordcount excluding bibliography and footnotes	**74,963**
Total number of entries in the index	**115**

How the entries are broken down:	
People (theorists, historians, filmmakers, politicians)	**24**
Historical figures/groups	**12**
Places (including exhibitions, buildings no longer in existence)	**15**
Acronyms (including variants, and translated terms used)	**2**
Key concepts and terms (including variants, and translated terms used)	**55**
Key debates	**4**
Key events	**3**

Step 28. Preparing for publication day

The moment you receive your box of author copies through the post is quite a special feeling. It is quite something to hold your published book in your hands for the very first time. Savour it, and the buzz of other people's excitement.

Take the opportunity a new publication affords to do some self-promotion. Contact your university librarian and see if they will promote your book. If you're on social media, post about it. If you can, arrange a simple competition to win a copy of your book. It will generate interest and is simple to arrange. Give a timeframe and pose a question. You could, for example, ask people to reply, explaining why they want to read your book or just ask them to like your social media post and then pick a name at random. It creates curiosity, which may lead to orders, whilst simultaneously engendering a feel-good factor. You can also do a book give-away in person, but don't feel you have to give away all your copies or do so all at once. Do what feels right to you.

Step 29. Organising your book launch

A new publication warrants a book launch to celebrate, as much as to promote it. For a first academic book, organising a book launch is a task that is likely to fall to you. If you have a bookshop nearby you can speak to them about the possibility, but this may come at a cost. Alternatively, if you are in a university post, talk with your School about organising a small book launch, inviting colleagues and students to it. Aside from perhaps a little bit of catering, you'll need a colleague to introduce you, and you'll need to prepare a short talk about your book – no more than 5 minutes – and be ready to take questions. Above all, this is about reaching a milestone and marking it with others.

Step 30. Celebrating

I'm a big advocate of celebrating achievement and doing so in a way that is authentic to you – that could be just with a book launch, it could be celebrating privately with family and friends. It might be that you are pressed for time, your publication coinciding with the demands of a new or proposed project, but do find a way to mark your achievement, as it is considerable. It will also be a while until your next book, and that's as it should be – **good books take time** – so enjoy this one when you can.

Congratulations on the publication of your book!

Review and Reflect

Everything in Context

When I started writing this guide, I wanted it to be about you and for you rather than a narrative of my experiences; there are other publications on writing your book that do take that approach. Yet, sharing is also good academic practice, and that is something I always want to encourage. To this end, the last pages of this book put my PhD to book journey in context.

My academic background is in German Studies, with a focus on cultural history. I have also worked on translation and in education. To date I've worked at the following universities: Cardiff, Leeds, Newcastle, Royal Holloway, University of London, and York, with forays outside of academia, including to the Welsh Joint Education Committee. I am currently based at the University of Leeds.

When I submitted my book proposal I was temping outside of academia. By the time I received my book contract I was working in higher education on the first of what would turn out to be a succession of temporary contracts. By the time my book was published, I was at another institution. That move proved a game-changer when it came to completing my manuscript, aided by different departmental practices, institutional cultures, and the crucial contract extension that gave me a summer free of job hunting in which to write.

Each of us will have a different journey, but it can help to see the route others took. To this end my PhD to book journey is encapsulated in the following diagram:

Contextualising the process: From viva to publication day

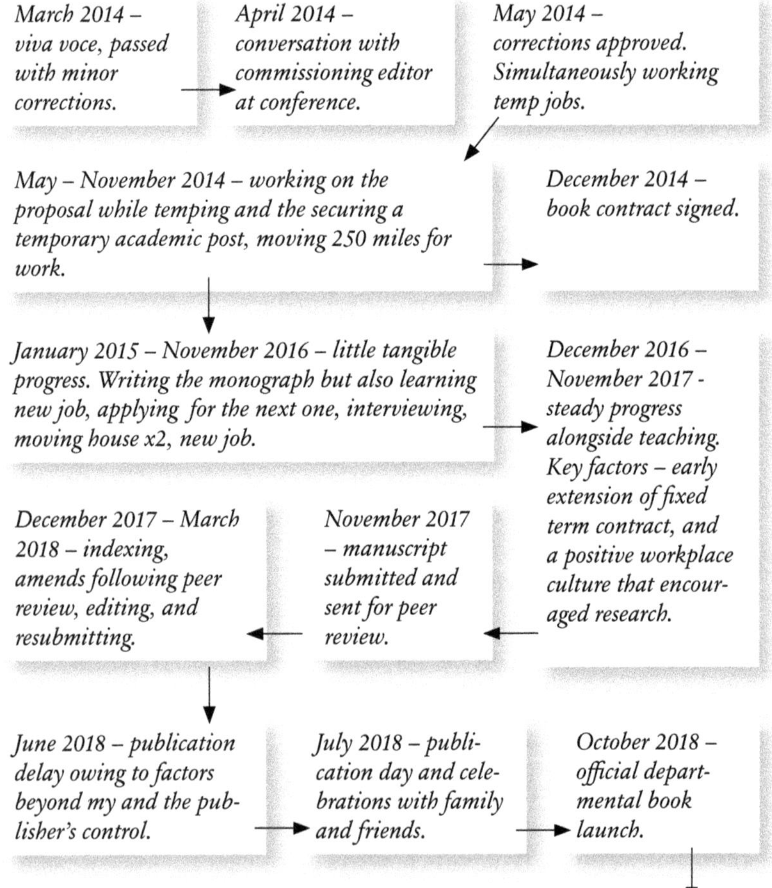

Acknowledgements

I enjoy writing acknowledgements. They are more than a list of thank-yous. I think of them as a way of recognising everyone's contribution, whilst simultaneously sharing with you, my reader, the story, and the process behind the book you are reading, of its development from concept to object. By sharing that level of detail, you get to see the book in a different way, and you gain an insight into my writing process. Given the subject of this book, doing so seems particularly apt.

If we start at the beginning, it is fitting that the first person I thank here, is Laurel Plapp, my commissioning editor at Peter Lang now twice over. It is thanks to Laurel that you are reading this book. As with so much in life serendipity plays a crucial role. Had Laurel and I not had a chance conversation back in March 2023, you would not now be reading this book, or even if we had, but if I had answered the question, 'how are you?' differently, and not followed it up with thoughts about this very topic, this book might never have come into being. I'd long since wanted to write about this topic, not just because of my own experience but also as a result of representing early career academics in various voluntary capacities. To this end, I extend my thanks here to what is now the University Council for Languages and to Women+ in German Studies. My involvement in both influenced my thinking and indirectly fed into the impetus behind this book.

Prior to that chance conversation with Laurel, this book was just a vague idea, its form indeterminate. A confluence of additional factors came into play at this point. When that conversation took place, I was mere days into a period of redundancy, and I wasn't sure what would happen next. I had not been looking to start a new book project, but I was entirely open to the idea, and it swiftly became something to focus on amidst all the uncertainty. At this point, I knew, all of a sudden, the form I wanted the book to take. It was the kind of flash of inspiration you imagine writers getting. I can, however, trace that vision back to the project I had just been involved with. It freed up my thinking, thereby allowing the inspiration for this book to emerge when the time was right. To this end my thanks go to Professor Emma Marsden, Dr Rachel Hawkes and colleagues for involving me in the then NCELP, now LDP team at the University of York.

I had only just begun working on this book, when I started a new role at the University of Leeds. I have Professor Jamie Stark and Professor Melanie Bell to thank for encouraging the development of this book, and for enabling me to work with our postdoctoral visiting fellows testing out activities in this book in a series of workshops. To those of you who took part in them, I thank you too. Each encounter not only helped in finessing the content, but the enthusiasm generated added to my writing momentum. With this in mind my thanks also go to the workshop participants at the W+IGS conference in Exeter in November 2023, who again put the activities to the test, and thanks also go to the conference organisers for giving me the opportunity in the first place.

I am grateful, too, to my early readers – Adaobi Muo, Matthew Treherne and Wei Zhou – who generously gave their time and expertise in commenting on the first draft. Your comments and suggestions made this a better book.

Friends and colleagues have also provided support, encouragement and enthusiasm in many a conversation along the way. My thanks to Alix Brodie-Wray, Emma Bowen, Louise Earnshaw, Corinne Painter, Ingrid Sharp and Shauna Walker, to name but a few.

I'd like to extend my gratitude here to my two reviewers for being generous with their time and their comments. The peer review process for this book really was an intellectually stimulating one, and it energised me as I returned to the manuscript. Your comments helped me to improve this book. Even in instances where I disagreed with a suggestion, your comments inspired me in one way or another, and in one guise or another they have made their way into the book. It was a truly enriching experience, for which I thank you and hope that we get the chance to work together someday.

Whilst the process of writing a book is dependent on the various people who help to develop it, just as important are the family who support you and help keep everything in perspective. Special thanks are owed to my in-laws, Jenny and Maurice for their boundless encouragement in everything I do. I thank you also for the use of your kitchen table at which much of the initial version of this book was sketched out. To my parents, Barbara and John, to my sister Gill, brother-in-law Phil, to my nephews Joel and Finn, thank you for your love and for being you. Without your support over the years, this book, nor the one that preceded it, would have come into being.

Last but by no means least, my thanks to Mark. Thank you for gifting me that notebook, specifying that one day I would have a project to capture in it – it turned out to be this. I thank you too, for the many discussions, questions, idea sharing, creative vision and graphic design skills that have helped me at various stages along the way. Most of all, I'd like to thank you for your love, and always being there, enriching my life in so many ways.

Further Reading

Caro, Sarah, *How to Publish Your PhD: A Practical Guide for the Humanities and Social Sciences* (London: Sage Publications Ltd, 2009)

Deblasio, Lisamarie, 'From PhD to Monograph: A Reflective Account of the Process', *Amicus Curiae,* 2/2, (2021), 255-260, DOI:10.14296/ac.v2i2.5257

Evans, Bec and Chris Smith, *Written: How to Keep Writing and Build a Habit That Lasts* (London: Icon Books, 2003)

Pope, Catherine, *How to Publish Your PhD* (Poole: Catherine Pope Limited, 2021)

Potter, Hilary, *Remembering Rosenstrasse: History, Memory, Identity in Contemporary Germany* (Oxford: Peter Lang, 2018)

Index

www.ingramcontent.com/pod-product-compliance
Ingram Content Group UK Ltd.
Pitfield, Milton Keynes, MK11 3LW, UK
UKHW021828270726
14058UKWH00001B/31